Down
Come the Leaves

Down

Come the Leaves

by HENRIETTA BANCROFT

illustrated by NONNY HOGROGIAN

Thomas Y. Crowell Company · New York

LET'S-READ-AND-FIND-OUT SCIENCE BOOKS

Editors: *DR. ROMA GANS*, Professor Emeritus of Childhood Education, Teachers College, Columbia University

DR. FRANKLYN M. BRANLEY, Chairman of The American Museum—Hayden Planetarium, consultant on science in elementary education

*AVAILABLE IN SPANISH

Down
Come the Leaves

LET'S
READ
AND
FIND
OUT

Leaves, leaves, leaves.
Down come the leaves:
    down, down, down.
Down come the leaves:
    red and yellow,
    orange and gold,
    green and brown.
Down come the leaves to the ground.

1

The wind blows the leaves.

It is time to rake them.
You rake, rake, and rake.
You make a big pile of leaves.

3

You walk in them.
You run in them.
You jump into the pile of leaves.
The leaves go swish as you jump.

Sometimes we burn the leaves.
The smoke smells good.
But it is better to save them.
Leaves break into little pieces.
They rot away.
They mix with the soil.
Trees and other plants use the old leaves for food.

Did you ever wonder why the leaves come down?
Leaves come down because their work is done.
Leaves make food. That is their work.
The food is for the plant.
Only green leaves can make food.
They make food in spring and summer.

8

9

Fall comes.
Work stops.
Down come the leaves.

Here are some leaves that come down in the fall.

Down come the leaves of the apple trees.
Down come the leaves of an elm tree.

Down come the leaves of a willow tree.

Down come the leaves of many other trees.
Here are some of them.

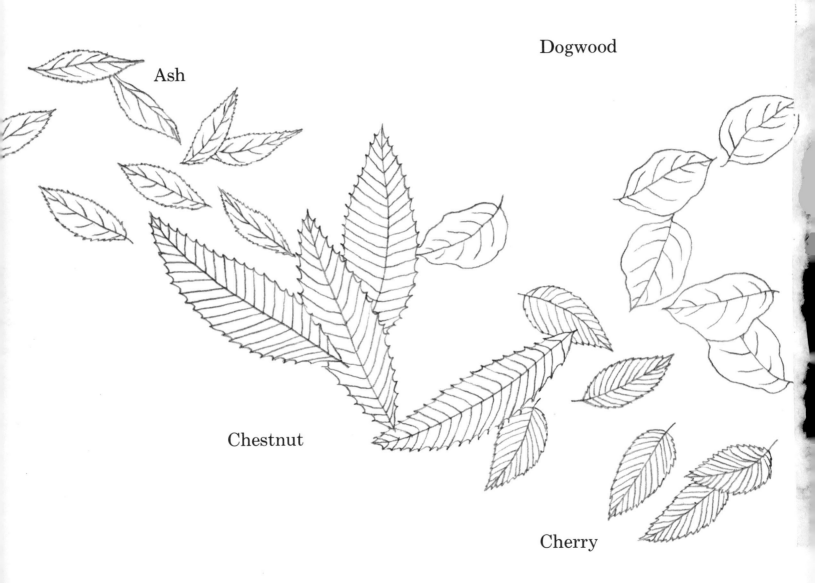

Dogwood

Ash

Chestnut

Cherry

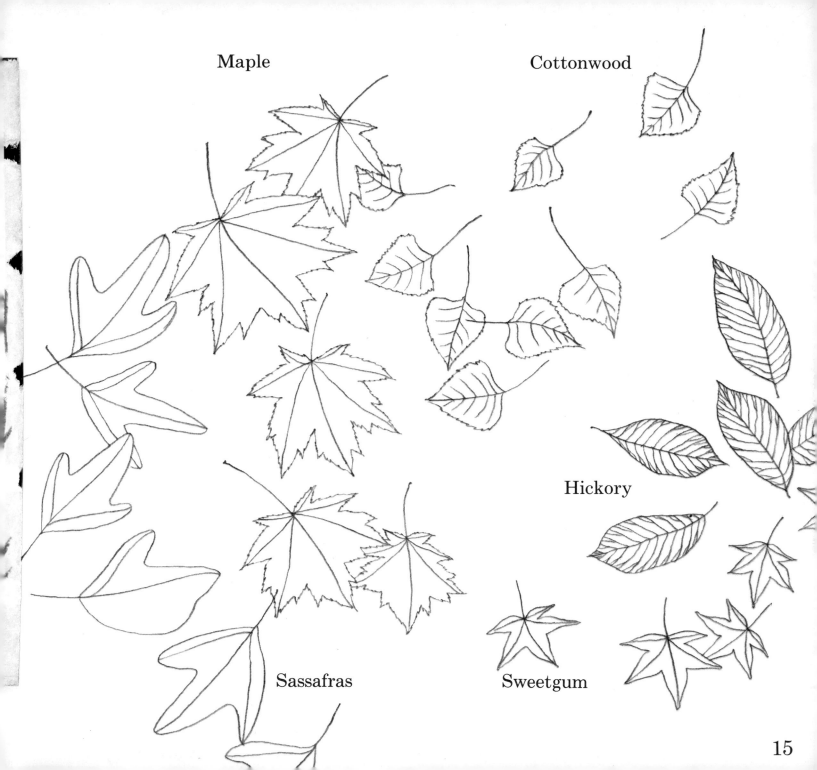

Maple

Cottonwood

Hickory

Sassafras

Sweetgum

15

Some trees keep their leaves all winter.

Here is a redwood tree. It has short, narrow leaves.

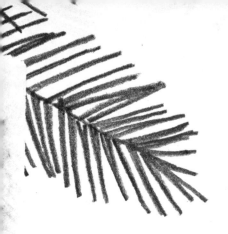

Here is a live oak tree. It has long, narrow leaves.
These trees keep their leaves all winter.

So do pine trees and spruce trees.

The leaves of pine trees and spruce trees are called needles.
All of these trees are green all winter.
They are evergreen trees.

Look at the leaves.
Some are big.
Some are little.
These are big leaves. They come from an oak tree.

These are little leaves. They come from a birch tree.

Some leaves are round, like these poplar leaves.

Some leaves are long and narrow. These come from a willow tree.

It is winter.

Many of the trees have no leaves.

Now the trees rest.

The trees rest all winter.

23

When spring comes, new leaves grow.
The new leaves were made last year.
They were inside buds all winter.
Now they come out of the winter buds.
Some are big. Some are little. Some are round. Some are long.

The leaves work all spring and all summer. They make food.

When the work is done, they fall to the ground.
Each year there are leaves to rake.

Each year there are leaves to run in and jump in.
Each year the leaves come down to the ground,
    red and yellow,
    orange and gold,
    green and brown.

Each year new leaves grow again.

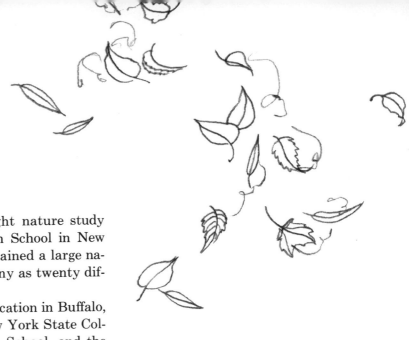

ABOUT THE AUTHOR

HENRIETTA NEWMAN BANCROFT taught nature study and elementary science at the Walden School in New York, where for many years she maintained a large nature room frequently filled with as many as twenty different kinds of animals.

Miss Bancroft received her early education in Buffalo, New York, and later attended the New York State College of Agriculture, Allegheny Nature School, and the University of Colorado. Besides traveling through the United States, she has visited many European countries and lived for a year in France and Switzerland.

ABOUT THE ILLUSTRATOR

NONNY HOGROGIAN is a native New Yorker. She graduated from Hunter College and has studied with Antonio Frasconi and Hodaka Yoshida. Miss Hogrogian is now concerned with the design, illustration, and publishing of children's books.